[Learn] Like A
Mind Reader

Jonathan **Pritchard**

Edition 1

ISBN-13: 978-0-9823708-3-4
ISBN-10: 0-9823708-3-0

[   ] Like A Mind Reader

[Learn] **Like A Mind Reader**

TABLE OF CONTENTS

Jonathan **Pritchard**

ACKNOWLEDGEMENTS

First, I'd like to thank Robert Yutzy. He was my high school debate teacher, and is uniquely responsible for helping me develop a way of thinking about problems that separates issues, and then looks for solutions. This approach has served me well, and I know it'll work for you. You can thank him later, too.

Second, I'd like to thank Helene Jacobsen & Danielle Price for their tireless work of reading, rereading, and reading some more. If the book makes sense, it's in no small part due to their efforts. Any typos or inconsistencies are purely my responsibility.

Lastly, I'd like to thank you, the reader. Wherever you are right now whether it's in a coffee shop, on a train, at work, on a beach, I'm glad to be there with you right now. Looking forward to spending some time together. Time's the only resource you'll never have again, so thanks for your vote of confidence that I'm worth an hour of your life.

Preface

I want to start this book with a piece of advice that my dad gave to me many years ago. It has served me well, and helped avoid many an unfortunate fate.

Keep this warning in the front of your mind as you read this book.

"Be careful what you get good at, son. You'll wind up doing it." **~Joseph Pritchard**

Use the knowledge inside this book to learn only those things that will make you happy. Remind yourself of my father's warning before you're tempted to do otherwise.

Introduction

T he **Matrix** is one of my favorite movies of all
time. Sure, it has its faults, but I saw it at an
impressionable age, and I was hooked forever. It has kung fu, computers, and explosions; what's
not to like?!

One of my favorite scenes has two main characters
(Neo & Trinity) on a rooftop looking at a helicopter,
and they need to escape the bad guys who are close behind them. Neo asks Trinity, "Can you fly that thing?"

She says, "Not yet," and makes a phone call to her
friend Tank. "Tank, I need a pilot program for a B212
helicopter. Hurry!" Tank types some keys, loading the
program for installation.

In the world of the movie, characters can have skills
directly installed to their brain. It's awesome.

Her eyes flutter for a second as everything she needs to
know about flying helicopters is downloaded straight

into her mind. It takes fewer than 5 seconds to load before she turns to look at Neo and says, "Let's go," as she strides to the helicopter.

Total elapsed time, 22 seconds.

I want that!

How badass would it be to download skills straight to your brain? You wouldn't have to read boring books, listen to lectures, waste countless hours (and years!) trying to remember useless crap.

Nope. Just download and BAM! You have it.

Since the day I saw that movie, I've been obsessed with figuring out how to learn skills as quickly as humanly possible. Who wouldn't want to learn how to fly a helicopter in 5 seconds?!

This skill of "learning how to learn" has been the single most important thing I've ever worked on, and it's contributed the most to my success.

People are amazed at the number of things I know how to do, (and do well). I'm constantly asked, "How in the world do you have the time to learn so much?!"

This book is the answer to that question.

I know how to "download" skills to my mind by using strategies learned from cutting edge psychology & neuroscience research. I don't waste years learning something; I can compress the learning curve to a couple months, a few weeks, or even a couple days in some cases.

Case in point. About 7 years ago I figured it was time I learn Kung Fu. I eventually found an instructor who wasn't going to waste my time teaching me how to shoot chi bullets from my fingertips, so I signed up. He and I knew right away that we were going to get along, and I've never looked back.

How long do you think it took for me to get my black belt? 2 years? 1 year? 9 months?

Answer is C: 9 months.

I know what you're thinking. "There's no way you could actually perform at a black belt level after such a short time."

Not true.

A couple months after getting my black belt, I had the opportunity to test skills with a guy who had his Krav Maga black belt for 12 years.

I threw him around like a ragdoll.

At the time, I had no idea who he was and it didn't matter. He was mine. (**Sidenote:** *This is not a claim that one system is better than another. One just is better.*) Maybe 13 months after I started training I was defending myself from a guy who had been at it for 12 years.

I successfully compressed more than a decade's experience into a single year.

"But, Jonathan," you say. "If you're learning how to do

all this stuff, aren't you worried about being a jack of all trades and a master of none? I know it takes forever to be the best at something. Let alone getting great at several things?"

Nope. Not at all.

With the strategies I'm about to show you, you'll be able to figure out what you need to learn, learn it, and apply it faster than you ever thought possible. You can quickly get into the top 20% of whatever you're learning about. And when you know more about a topic than 80% of people on the planet, you're the expert.

When you don't waste years learning the slow way, you suddenly have more time to learn more skills!

That's what makes this such a powerful concept. The better you get at learning, the faster you learn, which means you can learn more & more in less & less time.

When I was 13 I was juggling fire. At age 15 I was hammering nails up my nose. At age 18 I was eating fire.

Some skills are more valuable than others, and to this day I continue to teach myself whatever it is I want to learn. Whether it's for a new business opportunity, personal hobby, or experiment, I'm able to learn new things fast.

Most of the concepts we're going to cover are actually simple, but unless you've spent a lifetime searching for it (or going through this book) you wouldn't know it.

These are the exact same approaches I've used to teach myself Photoshop, video editing, copywriting, email marketing, website building, painting, magic tricks, and a whole bunch of useless bar bets.

No matter what the skill, the process of learning it remains the same. That's why you'll be able to learn math more quickly. Retain science information more easily. Learn a new language. I don't care what you want to learn. What I'm about to teach you will save you decades of wasted time.

The sky's the limit.

Jonathan **Pritchard**

Chapter 1:
Your Brain & You

That gray mass of cells you call a brain is basically a big electric slug that runs on about the same amount of energy as the lightbulb in your refrigerator (12 watts). Despite its relatively low energy needs, it uses 10x more energy (by weight) than any other part of your body.

It's also more complex than anything else we've ever found in the entire universe.

Everything you've ever thought, hoped, dreamed, or felt is contained in 3 pounds of neurons.

Pretty cool.

Despite being the most complex system in the universe, it's been forced to evolve some shortcuts. Remember, 12 watts isn't a lot of power, so your brain has to make the most out of what it gets. That means there are many opportunities for your brain to mess up. (Ever taken a shortcut that wound up costing you more time than you were trying to save?)

We take for granted how much work our brain does. We fool ourselves into thinking we know things we don't actually know, and feel confident with absolutely zero evidence to support that certainty.

Our brains & minds are tricky things, but that doesn't mean we can't make the most out of it.

We're going to dive under the surface of the conscious mind into the inner workings of your brain that you're not aware of. This will help you understand the systems at work, and how to make those systems work for you when it comes to learning a new skill.

We're going to rewire how you think about learning, significantly reduce your frustration, and increase your comprehension of new topics. You'll learn how to focus longer, retain information longer the first time you hear it, and master new concepts easily.

You'll see improvement across the board with the information you'll find inside these pages.

Welcome to your mind.

Happy learning.

Chapter 2:
Thoughts on Thinking

Most of us take for granted that our thoughts will always be there. Few understand the subtle differences between the different modes of thinking we use every single day to help us navigate reality.

A way to think about thinking is it's an awareness of attention, and there are two fundamental ways we can focus on something: Broad Focus & Narrow Focus.

Broad focus is a more relaxed state of awareness that allows your mind to wander. You're generally aware of reality, and what's going on around you, but you're not pinpointing any one area more than any other. Think of this like the "lantern" setting of your mind. It shines in all directions, but not very brightly.

In this state, you're free to float between, around, and through ideas. You make connections between 2 previously separate pieces of information or ideas. This is why daydreaming, or non-directed awareness is so important; this is where brand new ideas come from. It's a big picture mode of thinking that doesn't allow you to get lost in the detail. You can only see the big picture from up there.

Sometimes, however, you have to deal with details. Tiny, intricate, complex details. This requires sharp focus and sustained attention over a long period of time. This is where Narrow Focus really does a great job.

If Broad Focus is a lantern, Narrow Focus is a laser: full illumination, but in a very limited area.

Ever been so focused on something you completely ignored everything else around you? This is Narrow Focus. Your subconscious mind filters out all other sensory input in order to help you maintain full concentration on your work.

Whenever you're paying attention (to a conversation, your phone, a computer screen, etc.) you're in Narrow Focus mode. Most people never allow themselves to spend time in Broad Focus mode. We prefer to be constantly stimulated by magic screens that can tell us anything we've ever wanted to know. It's a powerful spell for sure, but constantly working in Narrow Focus doesn't allow you the space to come up with your own ideas.

Turns out, having the ability to engage your Broad Focus mode is absolutely essential if you want to learn something new.

Our modes are mutually exclusive.

You can't be in Broad & Narrow modes at the same time. It's an either/or set-up. Think of Narrow Mode as what you already know, and Broad Mode with what you want to know. Learning something new requires new connections, and Broad Mode is the only mode where that happens. Once the connections are made, they're reinforced with Narrow Mode.

This "Broad to Narrow Focus" approach will serve us well.

Chapter 3:
Broad Focus Mode & Creativity

Ever had someone's name right there, but the more you tried to remember it, the harder it was to think of it? Ever searched for a word you couldn't remember until it suddenly pops up out of nowhere 3 days later while you're in the shower?

If so, you've witnessed the genius of the subconscious mind. It doesn't play on your schedule, but it'll eventually tell you what you need to know.

The subconscious is the home of Broad Mode thinking. It's non-logical, non-linear, and it makes no damn sense. It's where your dreams live. On your own you'd never in a million years consciously think about going to school to be a butler, only to be shown up by a 10 year old in your class wearing a chicken suit.

But in dreamland, that's makes perfect sense.

27

Turns out, our brains are constantly in a dream state, but it's usually tethered to reality by what our sense organs are telling it about what's out there.

Contrarily, when you go to sleep your senses aren't providing as much information about what's "out there" so your brain is free to make associations and connections that have absolutely nothing to do with reality.

Artists have been using their dreams to create fantastic images and works of art by immediately recording their thoughts as they wake up.

It's not just artists; scientists & inventors have been known to leverage the power of their dream state to create insights.

Thomas Edison, (the guy who didn't fail but found 10,000 ways not to build a lightbulb) used an ingenious approach to come up with new ideas. He would hold a couple hefty ball bearings as he sat in a chair and thought of nothing. Since thinking of nothing is incredibly boring, he'd soon doze off. Inevitably his grip would relax and drop the ball bearings on the floor.

The loud noise would jerk him awake where he'd instantly be operating in Broad Focus mode, ready to record whatever new idea his brain was conjuring up.

Seeing how he was one of the most prolific inventors of all time, I'd have to say it's an approach that worked!

You may not use the same tactic, but it's definitely important to practice operating in Broad Focus mode. Just like any skill, it only gets better with repetition. Doing a little work every day will do more for you than a herculean effort once in awhile.

That's why when I was in college I never understood people who crammed for exams. My philosophy was if you didn't know it the night before the test, it was too late, regardless.

Turns out, one of the biggest secrets to learning something quickly is this: practice the skill of making time to learn a little bit each day. So the better you get at operating in whatever mode best serves you at the time you need it, the better you get at learning in general.

Chapter 4:
Enemy of Time

Since I just gave you one of the biggest secrets to learning quickly (creating time for learning every day), let's look at what's going to stop you from doing it.

Procrastination.

Procrastination will be your biggest enemy. It will fight you tooth & nail. It will lure you away with a siren's song of "there are better things to do with my time."

Learning how to fight procrastination is massively important because the most effective way to learn things is bit by bit over time. The sooner you start, the better off you are. The longer you wait to begin, the farther behind you'll be.

Success requires discipline, determination, and willpower which are much less common than procrastination. Show me 100 people and I bet one person might have self discipline. That's what makes procrastination so insidious; its effects filter out into every area of your life. You see your life falling apart, and you comfort yourself with little excuses here and there for why you're not to blame for it. Those excuses sound plausible, but you know they're just a lie whispered by procrastination designed to make you fall asleep.

WAKE UP! You're done with procrastination. That's why you're reading this book. You want to start making some big changes in your life. You want to learn some new skills, and I want to help you do it.

I'm going to tell you where the evil creature "procrastination" is birthed, and then give you a powerful weapon that you can use to slay the sworn enemy of progress once and for all.

Let's look to the humble amoeba. It's a single celled organism that will explain the secrets of motivation to us.

An amoeba will move towards food, and away from threats. There you go. That's the secret of motivation explained by an organism that doesn't even have a central nervous system.

Put in human terms, an amoeba moves towards pleasure, and away from pain.

And I know what you're thinking. You're thinking, "But Jonathan, I'm much more complex than an amoeba. It can't possibly be that simple for the shining pinnacle of evolution that is me."

You're right. Here's where you make it more complicated.

You move towards what you *think* will bring you pleasure, and away from what you *think* will bring you pain.

When you think about doing something you don't want to do (like going to the gym), your brain has increased activity in the areas associated with pain (the insular cortex). It's painful to anticipate doing something you don't want to do (even if it's good for you, like working out), so your brain (in a misguided attempt to make you feel better) looks for something else more pleasurable to do.

You feel better in the short term, but then you feel worse later by a measure of how much more time you've spent avoiding the thing you know you should be doing. Now, when you think about doing what you should be doing, you feel even worse than before so you put it off yet once again, and down the spiral of self loathing goes.

This shame spiral is the birth of the habit of procrastinating.

To understand it better, let's look at how habits are formed, how they work, and how to make them work for you.

Think about the first time you tried riding a bike. Fell over, right? There's a lot going on at the same time, and it's difficult to parse all the information you have to manage if you're just starting out.

Eventually, however, you learn to chunk more and

more pieces together until you simply think, "Go!" and you're pedaling into the sunset. It's the point where you no longer have to maintain narrow focus attention to an action that it begins to take shape as a habit.

Habits are time savers. They're shortcuts. They're robot response sequences that run below your conscious mind so you don't have to expend any more of that precious 12 Watts of power that your brain runs on so you have more energy for more important things.

This isn't a value statement; this is just how things are.

A fully fledged habit is built on 4 components.

First is the trigger. What's the context, action, situation, word, person, environment, etc., that immediately precedes the action? In the example above, it's sitting on the bike and putting your foot on the pedal. A powerful trigger for me is sitting down at the computer.

Second is the robot sequence. What's the routine of

behaviors, actions, thoughts, etc., that are performed below the level of conscious thought? This is the complex action of riding the bike without having to think about it. Or for me, when I sit down at the computer I'm almost instantly looking at Reddit.

Third is the payoff. What are you getting out of it? What's the reward? This is why procrastination is so enticing. It's an immediate reward of something more interesting than whatever else you're trying to avoid. That's why procrastination is so habit forming. It's a clear cut reward **now** to ignore that thing we'll get to **later**. Reddit lets me discover all kinds of (useless) interesting stuff!

Fourth is the narrative. What's your story around this habit? What do you tell yourself? What do you believe is true about the habit? You tell yourself you don't have the willpower to change. You believe your whole family is like this, so you lost the genetic lottery for procrastination. You believe your habit isn't harmful because you don't see any negative consequences. "I'll get back to writing in 20 minutes," you think. 3 hours later you're still on Reddit...

Change your story, and you change the whole sequence of habit. Allow yourself to reprogram your habits. You can make discipline & self control your new default habit.

The first part is truly believing you are capable of making the changes you need to form new habits.

The second part to changing habits is examine your triggers, and remove them. Maybe your cell phone buzzing is a trigger for you to stop studying and look at Facebook instead. Take your phone out of the equation. Put it in another room. Put it in your car. Try to reduce your exposure to triggers that signal old habits.

The third step is to install a new pattern of behavior. Picture the behavior you want instead as clearly as you can. Use as much detail as you can imagine. Really let your imagination run free, and try to feel, hear, smell, taste, and see everything about the new sequence you want to perform. Then, imagine a time in the future where you're faced with the old trigger, but see yourself responding with the new pattern instead of the old one.

The last part is resetting the reward. Give yourself a more compelling incentive than the old reward provides, and the new reward becomes much more motivating. Nothing will drive you to action better than loss aversion. We prefer to keep what we already have now, than to work for something we might not get in the future.

Use this to your advantage. Promise a friend that if you don't respond to a trigger the way you want to, you'll give them $20. You'll be surprised how motivated you'll be to keep that $20! You'll be rewarded with the happiness of keeping your money out of the hands of your friend, accomplishing a new pattern of behavior, and making positive change!

This is one of the fastest & most effective methods of establishing new behavioral habits.

Instead of getting momentary pleasure at putting something off, you'll get lasting satisfaction from putting in the hard work essential for success.

But I get it. Starting can be hard. It's painful.

Here's something interesting, though. Researchers found that not long after people started doing what they were trying to avoid, the insular cortex (the pain center) dramatically quieted down. This means that very soon after starting, the pain you were expecting, just isn't there.

Translation: the powerful weapon to defeating procrastination is to just start doing whatever it is you're avoiding in the first place.

You'll quickly discover it's not that bad, and you'll learn to associate the pleasure of taking action with doing something you didn't possible. This will drastically outweigh the imaginary pain caused by thinking about doing the thing.

If you don't believe me, and you're still procrastinating because you think the pain will continue past the start, here's a backup weapon. It's called the Pomodoro Technique.

The Pomodoro Technique uses a timer to limit the duration of Narrow Focus mode to 25 minutes.

Magically, knowing there's a preset time limit on how long a task is going to suck helps it suck less. Less suck equals less incentive to procrastinate.

Set the timer to 25 minutes, get to work, and when the timer goes off, relax completely. Once you've had a congratulatory cup of coffee and look out the window, do another 25 minute sprint.

Sprint and rest. Sprint and rest. Sprint and rest.

It's a fun change of pace, and it's a much better approach to managing your focus than slogging away for hours on end. That sounds like torture! No wonder you're trying to avoid it.

Wield the main weapon of "just do it" combined with the Pomodoro Technique, and you'll be unstoppable.

What's that? Procrastination is still breathing? You didn't slay the beast with the handy "just do it" attitude and Pomodoro technique? You want another weapon to make sure it's dead?

I got you.

Process versus Outcome

Imagine you needed to drive from New York to San Francisco. That's a hell of a trip, and it would take you days of sitting behind the wheel to get you there. You know you might be facing challenges like a flat tire, or busted radiator.

How much pain are you in right now just thinking about taking that imaginary trip?

That's procrastination!

You're thinking about the *outcome* which seems so far away. You'd rather live in a world where you could wish yourself to the other side of the country, so you don't start.

Procrastination!

You know what's easier, though? Focusing on staying between the lines. Maintaining your speed to match the traffic around you. Looking at the beautiful countryside as it slips past you.

You don't need to see your destination from where you are to start. Looking ahead just far enough to maintain movement will get you where you need to go.

Focus on the process of doing a thing rather than focusing on the desired outcome. Focus on driving, not the destination. If you're climbing Everest, think about the next step, not the top. Putting one foot in front of the other will get you to the top.

Very quickly the process required to complete a big project is taken over by the power of habit, and before you know it, you're done!

That's why the Pomodoro technique works so well. It frees you up to focus on the process of whatever it is you're doing without worrying about the outcome. You know whether or not you're done with the project, you'll be taking a break regardless. It tricks you out of focusing too much on the outcome.

Chapter 5:
Practice Makes...

How would you finish that saying? Would you say "perfect?"

I like to say, "Practice makes permanent."

If you practice the wrong thing, it doesn't matter how long you do it, it's still going to be wrong. Whatever you practice over and over again will become permanently ingrained in your mind. That's why it's so difficult to relearn a skill the "proper" way if you learned it the "wrong" way first. It can also lead you to perform a sequence of actions that are inappropriate for the current situation if you're not careful. I like to call that the "robot reaction." You respond in a pre-programmed way with no relationship to the current dynamic. Here's a great example of that.

There's a martial art story about a guy who trained knife defense non-stop. He would practice disarming his partner and then hand the knife back so they could practice again. Over and over they would practice. Then, one day in the real world he was assaulted by a guy with a knife. True to form, the martial artist disarmed his attacker, and then handed the knife right back to his would-be mugger without thinking about it.

Subconscious robot reaction!

Be careful how you learn things, and what you focus on building. See, when you first start working on a new skill, you're building new neural pathways in your brain. The path is there, but it's very faint. When you come back to it a second time, the path is worn in a little more. The connections get a little stronger. They're more resilient. Eventually the path is indelibly worn into your brain's architecture, and you no longer require conscious attention to execute the skill.

Think about learning to drive a car. At first you have a dim idea of what you need to do (keep the car between the lines), but there are so many details to keep track of, so it feels overwhelming. You can't possibly fathom this being easy, let alone fun!

You find yourself getting better and better at it, until you're happily texting and driving while eating a donut and drinking coffee.

Piece of cake.

So here's what you do. Bring the full power of Narrow Focus mode to whatever you want to learn for just 25 minutes. Turn off all other distractions, and completely shut out everything else. Your whole world is this new skill.

Then relax. Shift into Broad Focus mode. Let your subconscious find new connections. Let the pathways find their direction.

Then focus again.

It's a lot like breathing. You can't live by only breathing in **or** out. You have to do both. Focus, then relax. Focus, then relax.

Again, this is why cramming doesn't work. It's like trying to run a race by only breathing in. You're not leaving space for the other important stuff you need to do. . .

Focus on learning the right thing the right way, put in 25 minutes of concentrated effort, and then relax a while before doing it again. This will help you understand the material much better, and understanding is better than memorization any day.

Chapter 6: Memory

W e've made it this far without even talking about memory, so I guess now is as good a time as any to bring it up.

Memory is a skill, just like everything else. There are some tricks of the trade that can help you recall massive amounts of information, and I cover many of those in another book "**Perfect Recall.**" Here, however, we're going to dig into two types of memory that are important to us now.

Working Memory & Long Term Memory

If you know the color of the front door of your child-hood home you're accessing long term memory. If you've taken apart a wooden puzzle and you're trying to stay focused on how they came apart so you can put them back together again, you're using working memory.

Cognitive Scientist & Professor of Psychology, Anthony Barnhart explained working memory to me as a table where you put chunks of information that you're going to use soon. It's a relatively small table top so it can only accommodate 4 to 7 pieces. Anything more than that, and the pieces you put down first start getting pushed off the edge by the new items.

Ever tried to remember a license plate number from a car that's speeding off? Difficult, right? That's because your mind is constantly trying to prioritize information as you perceive new bits of information. That's why you close your eyes when you're trying to remember things long enough to write them down; it helps shut out the flood of new details that would push the important stuff off the table.

Or you could think of it like a dry erase board with ink that only lasts for a short time. You can almost watch what you've written fade away as you write something new. That's working memory.

Fun Fact: Anthony also told me that (unofficially) there was a study looking into working memory, and the researchers found an interesting correlation between the size of a person's working memory & long term success. People with higher functioning working memories were more successful across the board. Unfortunately, working memory seems to be non-responsive to training or efforts to improve it. What you're born with is what you have. Money you spent on all those brain training apps is wasted. They only get you better at those specific exercises; the skills don't seem to transfer to other situations. Sorry!

If working memory is a table top with room for 7 items, long term memory is like a giant warehouse with a grass floor.

Once you've built something on the table that you want to keep for later, you walk to a new part of the warehouse and put it on the shelf. You leave a faint path in the grass when you do that, and if you don't walk the path again it tends to fade away pretty quickly. If you want to be able to find your way back, you have to walk the path several times in a short period so you wear a deeper groove in the grass. Soon it'll be a clear cut channel that will remain even if you don't go back for awhile.

The warehouse is gigantic. You can't even conceive how much room there is in there. You literally couldn't find the end of it if you tried; there's space for billions (with a B) of pieces of information. The problem, however, is details can get so cluttered that they hide where earlier memories are located. If you can't find the memory, even if it's there, it's no different as if it weren't there in the first place.

Fun Fact: This is the idea behind repressed memories, but it's 99.9% more likely that repressed memories are the result of false memories being installed under the guise of "helpful" hypnosis sessions. For a more in-depth look into the phenomenon of false memories, check out Elizabeth Loftus' work. It'll blow your mind.

The process of refreshing associations to ensure your pathway remains intact is called "spaced repetition." When you're first learning something, it's useful to re-visit daily, and sometimes multiple times a day. Once you have it down, you can increase the time between recall to a day or so. Once you have it down on a daily scale, you can increase the delay to a couple days. This slow and steady pace is much more effective than trying to cram it all in during one session. The space between practice sessions gives your subconscious mind time to clear out the mental junk, and reinforce the connections you're using more often.

Geographic and Spatial Memory

Think back thousands and thousands of years to the time when humans were primarily hunter/gatherers. It would be a matter of life and death to know where you could find water. Our brains evolved to be incredibly adept at remembering where valuable resources are in a given geography.

Back then our lives didn't depend on remembering someone's name or a random number, but knowing where a watering hole is sure mattered!

That's why when you walk through a house, you instantly catalogue thousands and thousands of pieces of information ranging from where the exits are, furniture placement, position of appliances, and so on. We're phenomenally good at recalling details about places. It's a skill that's hardwired into our minds.

That's why I used the metaphor of the infinite warehouse of memories. Our minds already work that way. We care more about where things are and how they look more than what they mean or their abstract idea.

This means visualizing information helps you retain it. The more ludicrous the image, the better. The more absurd the size, the better. The more numerous the subject, the better. If you can translate an abstract idea into a nonsense physical thing in your mind's eye, you're tapping into your ancient evolutionary disposition for placement & appearance to improve the likelihood you'll remember it later.

Surprisingly, memory & recall is only a part of learning. Figuring out what's important, discerning meaningful relationships between those important parts, etc are all just as valuable, if not more so, but memory is absolutely crucial.

There's a lot more we could cover about memory, but one piece we can't ignore is how important it is to give your mind time to clear out the junk.

Jonathan **Pritchard**

Chapter 7:
How Do We Clear
the Mental Clutter?

D ue to regular metabolic functions, there's a lot of crap that builds up in our brain after sustained cognitive load. These byproducts will interfere with regular cognitive functions if they're left in place. So how do our bodies clear it out?

When we sleep, our brains contract just a bit which allows fresh neural fluid to flow in and around our brain cells. This washes away what's not supposed to be there, and gives the connections that are supposed to be there the space they need to grow stronger.

Sounds like science fiction, but it's 100% true!

That's why your ability to make decisions degrades so drastically when you've been awake too long. You start making bad choices without even knowing it. (Or you just don't care.) Also, prolonged bouts of too little sleep can have severe long term health consequences.

Beauty sleep isn't just for your face!

In addition to sweeping out the biological byproducts of thinking, sleep also gives our minds an opportunity to go through the day's events, thoughts, ideas, etc. and evaluate them for importance. Important stuff is reinforced. Everything else gets torn down.

New ideas are formed during this process, too. Since your conscious mind is completely dormant, your dreaming mind is freed to make those non-linear associations I mentioned earlier.

Research has shown that studying something just before going to sleep can help you recall that information more easily with less effort. Neat hack.

Chapter 8:
Chunks

Remember how I talked about working memory having space for an upper limit of 7(ish) pieces of information? Those pieces are called chunks. We're going to dig into how chunks are created (not all are created equal!), how to use them, and how chunks can help you learn faster across the board.

When you're learning a completely new skill, concept, ability, language, etc it can be confusing. All the pieces are floating around with no context, and no way for you to make sense of what you're looking at.

Chunking is the process of clicking those random pieces of information with each other and other bits of information you know already.

Think about breaking each topic or skill into the smallest units of information you can understand. These are the beginning chunks that you have to lock into your mind.

65

Example: In juggling, the 2 smallest skills are learning how to 1) throw a ball & 2) catch the ball. "Tossing" would be your first chunk; it's an idea that combines the throw & catch part of the equation.

Just like a computer's compression algorithm, chunking simplifies several details by locking them into a single unit.

Before long you move from "throw, catch, throw, catch, throw, catch. . ." to "toss, toss, toss, toss, toss, toss. . ." and then you move to "Basic cascade to Mill's Mess to reverse shower. . ." (Fancy juggling terms.) Each chunk you create prepares you for the next level of refinement.

Your job as a MetaLearner (someone who learns how to learn) is to parse the most fundamental pieces of information, figure out which ones appear most frequently, chunk those, and then build off that foundation with the less common details. This process ensures you provide maximum connection to the new information which, in turn, maximizes long term recall.

This is why it's easier for you to remember the name of someone who has the same name as someone you already know. It's easier to find a meaningful relationship to information you know already. We can never remember anything without relating it to something we know already. This is why learning a new written language can be so difficult; the characters exist completely outside our previous experience, and are therefore outside our mental context.

First you learn to identify letters. Then you figure out how letters chunk together to form words. Then you can manipulate how words fit together to form sentences. Sentences to paragraphs. Paragraphs to books. Books to volumes to shelves to sections to libraries to networks, and so on. Chunk, chunk, chunk.

This process of chunking (creating mental connections, and evaluating new information for relevance) is a function of Narrow Focus mode attention. Chunking is the process of your brain building neurological pathways that encode a particular piece of information at higher and higher levels of abstraction. The better you get at a skill, the fewer neurons are needed to trigger a whole cascade of ideas/actions/responses/ etc. Each level of chunking encodes more and more information as easily as when you were learning at the earlier level. Pretty cool.

How do chunks actually click together? Glad you asked.

Let's go back to the example of learning how to juggle. Before you attempt your first toss, you would probably watch some juggling videos on YouTube. You'd watch people who knew how to juggle, and try to imagine how it would feel for you to do what you're seeing them do. You eventually get bored of watching, so you go outside to try it yourself.

At first you only focus on throwing the ball from one hand to the other. You really pay attention to how it feels as the ball leaves your hand, and you get immediate feedback on the quality of the throw. "That throw was a little too far forward, and not high enough. Ok." This immediate feedback helps your mind encode a chunk that evaluates that kinesthetic awareness as "good toss" or "bad toss."

Notice we haven't even gotten to evaluating the other half of the toss: catches.

It might seem like overkill to spend this much time on the basics. Ironically, however, spending more time on the basics will help you learn faster in the long run than glossing over the foundation so you can "get to the cool stuff." The stuff that comes later is only as solid as the foundation it's built on. That's why figuring it out for yourself, and understanding how and why it all clicks together will serve you much better than breezing through in a "do as I do without thinking" approach.

It's the difference between being able to navigate for yourself with a compass and the stars, or having GPS tell you where to go. Both will get you where you want to go, but one is installed in your own understanding and the other doesn't work without batteries.

To continue the juggling example, let's now focus on what's going on in your mind as you practice. This is the same for any kind of mental effort; whether you're trying to encode formulas, languages, or any other kind of mental information.

As I touched on earlier, the first step is to actually focus on what you're trying to learn. No distractions. Turn off your cell phone. Turn off desktop notifications. Background distractions mean part of your mental capacity is spent on maintaining awareness of something other than what you're trying to learn. Say it's 20% background noise. That means it's going to take 20% longer to learn whatever you're trying to learn. Do yourself a favor and get rid of as many distractions as you can.

The next step to creating a chunk is to really get your mind around the basic idea you're trying to understand. Create connections. Make associations to stuff you know already. For example, when I'm learning a new language, I associate the words for "You, me, them" to space. "You" is in front of me. "Me" is me. "Them" is off to my left. I imagine 3 points in physical space in a way that's similar to the physical location of the people I'd be referring to. That way, when I imagine the point of the triangle (a concept I'm already familiar with), it will trigger the association with the

[Learn] **Like A Mind Reader**

correct word.

No matter what the association is, once it finally locks into place you can be said to understand the concept. Once you understand the concept, you can start chunking information and build from there.

> **Caution:** Knowledge does not equal understanding. Imagine seeing a magic trick. You're completely baffled, and you want to know how it works. Somehow you get the magician to show you how it works. Now you have knowledge of how the trick works, but you don't understand why it works. Further, you'll probably forget the basic knowledge soon, too since it lacks relationship to anything else you know. Thinking you understand a trick when you barely have the knowledge of how it works is the foundation of fooling yourself. This isn't limited to magic, however. It happens all the time in every topic. This is precisely why something makes sense when an expert is explaining it, but then you get confused when you try to explain it to your friend later.

Seeing is different than understanding. Understanding is different than doing. We human creatures learn best through doing.

Once you understand something, the next step is working out its broader context. Figure out how it relates to what you know already. Figure out how it doesn't relate to some things. Find where it's useful. Find where it isn't.

This is where you discover a hammer is great for putting a nail through 2 pieces of wood, but not so good at making 2 pieces of wood from one. It's all about context!

Playing with context allows you to find multiple ways to get to the same piece of information instead of only relying on one way to find it in your memory. The more connections and pathways you have to a technique / piece of information / memory, the more useful it will be to you.

Chapter 9:
Knowing versus Thinking

So how do we keep from fooling ourselves into thinking we know something when we really don't? How do we know when we really know something?

Say you're trying to learn some complex economics ideas. There were a bunch of unfamiliar terms, big picture ideas, names, dates, and so on. What do you do? If you're like most people, you'd probably reread the information in an attempt to shove it farther into your mind. Unfortunately, this winds up being counterproductive.

Instead of diving right back into the information, try this. Try to consciously bring to mind as many details as you can before you go through the chapter again. Once you reach the end, try to recall as much as you can before rereading again.

This approach will help you learn so much faster than

just reading the same stuff over and over again. Think of it like this. Reading the information is the expert explaining it to you, so it makes perfect sense. Recalling the details is you trying to explain it to your friend. Each time you explain it to your friend, you'll figure out what you actually know, and what you're still fuzzy on.

Then, when you go back to the expert, they'll help you fill in the gaps & reinforce the stuff you've gotten right. Then you go back and explain it to your friend, but this time it's even more coherent.

Or, to use the warehouse analogy: you're walking to the information and back again. There, and back again. There and back again instead of just staying put. Remaining stationary doesn't wear a path in the grass.

This process of read, recall, reread is an amazingly effective technique to encode new information into your memory. It illustrates why your active engagement with the information is essential. Passive learning gets you nowhere.

Meta-tip: Since we've been talking about context of information and how it related to chunking, let's talk about context in another way: physical space. If you always study in a particular room, you might remember the information in that room, but if you go somewhere new you might lack many of the physical & environmental cues you've unknowingly encoded along with the information.

Combat this flaw by engaging in recall practice in a variety of contexts (physical, mental, emotional, etc.). The more contexts you practice your chunk relationships, the more powerfully they will be locked into your memory.

Think of it like a spider web. Each strand is weak by itself, but put enough strands together, and you'll be surprised how strong they are.

Each context reinforces the other, and creates stronger connections.

Chapter 10:
How & Why

When you're approaching a new skill you're often focused on the "how." How to hit a baseball. How to speak another language. How to do this, how to do that.

True understanding comes from knowing how, and then WHY you're doing it the way you are.

Think about learning martial arts. First you learn how to block. How to punch. How to move around without compromising your balance.

Then you start applying your newfound "how" knowledge in a safe setting known as sparring with your training partners. There's minimal resistance. It's low stakes. You're allowed to cultivate experiential knowledge without worrying about getting knocked out by your opponent.

You're both helping each other learn. You're each other's training partners.

This direct application of the "how" helps you understand the "why" behind it. Every skill has a why behind the way it's done, and the more you put the how into practice, the faster you'll see the why.

Once you grasp the why of a technique or skill, your understanding (and capacity to learn more) deepens. This is because your mind has done the hard work of forming neural pathways and interconnections itself instead of just listening to what your teacher tells you.

Fighter pilots don't just read books about dogfights and instantly know everything about air combat. They have to try it. Experiment with it in practice.

They take the time in training to use their conscious mind to explore the how of flying, in order to touch the why.

Once the why is fully understood through repeated experience in a variety of contexts, the conscious mind is no longer needed to perform complex movements or procedures.

In fact, the conscious mind can actively interfere with your ability to perform at maximum effectiveness. Imagine a martial artist thinking about punching instead of instinctively performing the technique.

If you don't fixate on the how, you'll maintain the ability to constantly evaluate new information in novel ways. This contributes to a better understanding of the why of the material.

Chapter 11:
Magic of Metaphor

I think almost entirely in pictures. It's one of my biggest strengths, and biggest weaknesses.

It's a weakness because it can sometimes take me days to translate an image into a coherent idea that I can communicate with words. That's the main reason I took debate six semesters in high school, and continued to pursue it in college.

Competitive debate forced me into a situation where I couldn't rely on drawing a picture to get my point across. Instead, I'd have to quickly interpret my first impression (which would be in the form of an image or picture), as a logically structured verbal argument for an idea.

Thinking entirely in pictures was a benefit because an image is a much denser medium for encoding information. And as we covered in the section on geographical and spatial memory, our brains have evolved to recognize how things look and where they really are, moreso than thinking about the word we use to describe all that.

This is why metaphors and analogies are so useful when you're learning something. Metaphors are methods of connecting disparate ideas or things, and you can use imagery to create those associations.

Since our minds recall visual information easier than abstract symbols like letters and numbers, you can create visual mental models for complex ideas that can serve you well.

As you learn more about the topic, your metaphors can get more complex, or you can throw them away completely because you've immersed yourself completely into how it actually is instead of relating to the material by way of how it's similar to something else.

Example: In 9th grade chemistry class I learned about covalent & ionic bonds that form the basis for all molecules. One type of bond (covalent) shares electrons between atoms, and the other bond (ionic) means one atom steals the electron from the other atom. I immediately thought of James Bond. He's a master at theft and espionage, so I imagined Sean Connery introducing himself as, "Bond. Ionic Bond."

As of the time I'm writing this, it's been 18 years since that class and I still remember that image. That's how powerful visual metaphors can be.

Just like with all tools, however, there are certain dangers to be aware of. All metaphors will break down at some point where they no longer apply, so only use the metaphor as long as it's useful. Don't try to carry the metaphor beyond its purpose.

Also, don't let your rigid logical mind get in the way. Metaphors (visual or otherwise) don't have to make sense; they just have to work. In fact, the more ridiculous the association, the more likely you are to remember it later. It's merely a tool for you to create mental connections between two pieces of information.

Chapter 12:
But I'm So Busy

With all this talk about how the mind works, how to improve your memory, chunking, and so on, we've completely ignored one of the biggest influencers on how quickly you can learn: you're just too damn busy for all this stuff.

Frankly, I'm amazed you've gotten this far! You have a million things you could be doing, and you're choosing to read the words I've spent weeks typing. Very flattering, thank you.

But I get it. Life is busy. Every moment is already spoken for. Seems like you can't find a spare 5 minutes just to take a breath, much less dedicate a whole chunk of time to something new.

That's why I want to talk about opportunity cost, and the real price of saying "Yes."

Most of my life has been lived as an adventure. "Whatever makes for a better story" has been my go-to mantra for as long as I can remember.

And I let it destroy my life.

When we talk about decision making, there's a lot of ink spent on deciding between two possible outcomes. When you choose one path, it's at the cost of being able to pursue the other path.

Those two choices are both abstract future possibilities.

But something we don't talk about much is how you're often not making a choice between 2 hypothetical outcomes. Sometimes you're making a choice between how things are right now, and how they could be.

The opportunity to have what you want is at the cost of everything you have already.

Radical Honesty Time

Not many people know I used to be married.

Past tense.

We met when we both worked at Disney World, so we were both heavily under the "Happily Ever After" magic spell of the happiest place on Earth.

After several years of marriage, there was an opportunity to be with someone who wasn't my wife.

I said yes.

The cost of that opportunity was the marriage, my friendships with her whole family, the stability of 2 incomes, all the wedding gifts, the trust of my friends, and I could go on outlining what that single choice cost me.

Point being, when you're making a choice, it's not always between two possible outcomes. It's often between a possible outcome and how things actually are right now.

Negative to a Positive

My example happens to be negative, but it doesn't always have to be. I wanted to share that story because it outlines how I've learned some of these lessons the hard way; I'm not perfect.

But the question stays the same.

What are you saying yes to right now that's costing you everything?

There are things you're saying yes to right now that are at the expense of having the opportunity to have everything you've ever wanted. It's up to you to find out what those things are, and learn how to say no to them.

Unlimited Power

When you say no, you're not just deciding against something; you're saying yes to what you truly want.

If you want success, you're going to have to say no to a lot of things you might enjoy. Otherwise, your life quickly fills up with obligations, things, people, and time wasters that aren't moving you closer to where you want to be.

Same Coin

So you can see, saying yes & no are 2 sides of the same coin. When you say yes to something, you're saying no to everything else. When you say no to something you're saying yes to something else.

Choosing what you say yes & no to is the single act that dictates how your life plays out. It can be saying yes or no to jobs, houses, relationships, hobbies, etc. It can be anything.

And it all costs you dearly.

That's why success and failure costs everything you have.

When you tell me "I'm too busy to learn something new", I hear you actually saying "I've said yes to a whole bunch of crap that's slowly suffocating me, and strangling my ability to enjoy anything in life."

You can fool yourself, but you're not getting one by me. (I'm a mind reader, remember!)

Saying Yes to Learning

So you've said no to enough of the trivial stuff that's not doing anything for you, so there's now space for you to learn something new. Now what? What are some strategies that will help you stay on track?

Write It Down

No matter what you're working on, there are going to be key things you can do to move your skills forward. Whatever they are, write them down the night before you're going to work on them.

This does 2 things:
First, it allows your conscious mind to relax. How often are you kept up all night thinking about the things you need to do tomorrow? That's your mind trying not to forget something important. Once you write it down your mind can relax because it knows the detail is in a place you can come back to when you wake up.

Second, it allows your non-conscious mind (all the parts of your mind that aren't under your direct influence) to start figuring out how you're going to accomplish what you want to do tomorrow. It's like you're priming the mental pump. You've gotten the conscious mind out of the way, and now the non-conscious mind has the space to really get to work.

Use A Journal

For the practice of nightly writing, I like to use a physical journal. Sure, Google Keep or Evernote are infinitely searchable, but there's nothing like using good old pen & paper to program your mind.

Your mind tends to change to fit the shape of the digital journal you're using, whereas the process of using pen & paper seems to encode the information into your mind in a way that digital mediums don't do.

Before long you'll find yourself getting better and better at remembering what you've written, figuring out how to use it more effectively, and judging what you can accomplish in the time you've set aside for learning.

Plus, make sure you set a firm deadline for yourself when you're writing all your ideas. Having a set quit time helps you maintain healthy boundaries, and prevents mental drifting. Again, this is one of the beauties of the Pomodoro technique.

When I was in college I almost never studied past 7pm. That made sure I had time to enjoy hanging out with my friends, and helped keep study time from taking over my whole life. Consequently, I had a great experience in college while graduating with good grades!

Greens First
Another way to get the most out of your learning time is to eat your greens first.

I hate spinach. I hate leafy greens. But I know they're good for me, so I'll load my plate with them, and make sure to eat those first. That way I get the stuff I don't like out of the way first, and end my meal with whatever I like the most.

Same goes for your studying.

Whatever you don't like doing, work on that first. If it's important, work on that too. Get the stuff you have to do done first, and then you can enjoy whatever comes after that.

As soon as I wake up, I immediately work on the most important thing in my life: my kung fu practice. I know if I do it right away, the rest of the day will go well. If I let my day dictate my choices, though, I wind up not doing my practice, and my life winds up falling apart.

Maintain focus on what's important & most essential. Work on that first, and then play with the time you have left.

Chapter 13:
Ultimate Test

Whether you're in junior high, high school, college, or working on a new business certification, you're probably going to be tested on the material you're learning.

Even if you're learning a new language for fun, your test takes the shape of trying to communicate with another person.

That's why I want to explore a couple strategies for successful test taking. This is one of the main ways I got good grades in high school. I wasn't a whiz at the information; I got good at taking tests. These are some of the tricks I used.

Study in Multiple Locations

As I already touched on in the Meta-Tip in the "Knowing versus Thinking" Chapter, location-specific recall can seriously affect your ability to remember crucial information if you've only studied in one place. If you only ever study in your room, you might have trouble remembering details when you're in the exam room.

Answer-Only Attention

This was especially handy in high school where most of the test questions came straight from our daily homework. That's a supremely lazy method of teaching (and a specious use of the word "teaching" too), but it's a common practice.

Here's what I did. When it came time to study for the test, I'd only look at the question and correct answer. I wouldn't try to digest the how, why, or anything else.

What I was doing was establishing an "If-then" pattern recognition system. "If I see question X, then answer Y."

During the test, I'd see the question, and only one choice would feel vaguely familiar.

I wouldn't even have to know what the right answer meant; just that it was the one that felt familiar.

Scan & Strain

This approach helps you avoid running out of time because you got stuck on challenging questions.

When you get your test, the first thing you should do is scan all the questions. Keep an eye out for any that are going to give you problems.

Once you have your broad overview, look more closely at the difficult problems; the ones you're really going to have to expend effort on. This is the strain part.

When you feel yourself getting stuck on it, immediately switch to easy questions.

This does a couple things.

First, it allows you to revamp your confidence. It keeps you from getting stuck in a mental loop of "This is too difficult, I'm never going to get this, because it's too tough. . ."

Second, it puts the difficult problem on the back burner where your subconscious can start pulling non-logical associations together in a bid to solve it for you before you get back. This way your conscious mind works on the easy problems, and your subconscious works on the tough problems at the same time. Neat, right?

Third, it gives you a chance to recognize the answer to the tough problem inside an easier one. I can't tell you how many times I've answered an easy problem that gave me the piece I was missing to the tough question. If I hadn't started with the tough question first, I would have denied my broad focus mode the chance to recognize it for me.

So if you get stuck, give yourself permission to try something else for awhile before coming back. Scan, strain, return, and repeat.

Power of Reframing

What you choose to tell yourself about an experience influences how you experience it. This is a lesson I learned through public speaking.

Standing in front of a group of people and speaking is

one of the number one fears people have.

If that's you, just the thought of a presentation can freak you out. Your breathing gets shallow, your palms get sweaty, you stomach feels like it's full of lightning, and you'd do anything to make it stop.

This is the epitome of being nervous.

Now, think about a time you went on a first date with someone you really liked. I bet your breathing was shallow. Your hands were sweaty. Your stomach was full of lightning.

And you loved it.

This is what I mean about the power of reframing. The physiological responses are exactly the same in both situations, but it's what you tell yourself they **mean** that makes the difference between a great experience and horrible one.

People ask me all the time if I get nervous before going on stage. I tell them my heart rate still increases. My breathing still gets shallow. My hands still get sweaty.

And it's because I'm excited to get out there and have fun with 2,000 of my new best friends. (This is exactly what I did before I walked out on stage in front of millions of people for America's Got Talent. I told myself, "You're excited. This is what you do. This is what you've worked your whole life to do." Then I went out there and crushed it.)

That's what I mean when I say what you tell yourself a situation means is what dictates how you experience it.

When it comes to test time, tell yourself you're excited to do a great job; don't tell yourself you're freaked out.

Face Your Fear

Nothing will freak you out worse than failing a test. Especially if you've gone your whole life believing that you have to get good grades in high school so you'll get into a good college so you can graduate with honors so you can get a great job afterwards.

With that much pressure on one test, no wonder you're freaked out! If you're that freaked out, it would be twice as amazing if you didn't flunk it.

If you're a surgeon, I'd imagine it's difficult to do a good job if someone is constantly screaming at you to do a good job. . . Give yourself permission to stop screaming at yourself to be perfect.

The cool thing is, even if you barely pass a test, it doesn't matter in the grand scheme of things. You know what they call someone who got D's in medical school? Doctor.

Once you realize that success in life is rarely predicated on a single moment, the weight you place on each decision becomes so much lighter. With that relaxed attitude, you Jedi mind trick yourself into a headspace where excellence flows easily.

This reminds me of the samurai saying, "Matters of great concern should be treated lightly. Matters of small concern should be treated seriously." Be a samurai.

103

Chapter 14:
Progression Multiplier

So far we've talked about ways to learn on your own & bootstrap your progress. I've saved the best for last.

What's the secret weapon I've used to catapult my way to the top of the mountain in several areas?

I'll give you a hint: I'm doing it for you right now. . .

Answer: Find a mentor.

That's it. That's the ultimate secret to learning anything as fast as humanly possible. Sure, you can learn from books. I grew up reading magic books and learned most of my foundational knowledge from reading.

But when I met my mentor, everything changed.

James Randi Educational Foundation

It was my second semester at Berea College, and I saw

a poster announcing an upcoming lecture by James "the Amazing" Randi. This was a big deal.

Randi is a legend in the world of magic. He was on "Happy Days." He was on Carson's "Tonight Show" an astounding 33 times. He battled Uri Geller in the 70's, and he's responsible for the legendary magic duo "Penn & Teller."

I had to meet him.

I figured out who was organizing Randi's time on campus, and hounded him. "I have to meet this guy! You know I do magic; he's a legend! What can I do?!"

Success! My job was to walk him from the hotel on campus over to the luncheon where he would then meet his next escort to the next appointment.

That meant I had about 10 minutes of uninterrupted time.

I don't remember what all I said, but it seemed to work. I wound up cutting classes for the next two days as we hung out for hours talking magic theory, science, perception, and all things critical thinking.

He would explain bizarre experiments he set up, and then ask me what I thought he was testing. I'd give my answer and he'd let me know whether I was right or wrong. Then he would give me another thought problem.

There was a moment that defined the rest of my life. I remember thinking, "If I wait for him to ask me to the prom, I'm going to be left at home crying, so I'll have to do it myself."

I gathered all the courage I could muster and said, "Randi, do you need any help at the Foundation? I'm sure I can set something up through the college that would count as credit, get some funding, and it wouldn't cost you much."

He thought for a moment and said, "You're hired!"

My next 4 summers were spent down in Ft. Lauderdale living 2 miles off the beach. My job was to handle applications for his Million Dollar Challenge.

It was a "put your money where your mouth is" challenge to anyone claiming to have supernatural abilities, like being able to read minds. The applicant's job was to tell us what they could do, under what circumstances, and with what accuracy.

Based on that information, I'd work with Randi to develop a double blind pass/fail test of each person's "ability."

Eventually I saw all the ways people were trying to scam their way to the million dollars, and thought, "Hell, I can do that better than they can!" and so my mentalism career was born.

Every day I spent at the foundation was basically like a year's worth of reading compressed into 24 hours. Randi is such a wealth of information and experience that my understanding of critical thinking, skepticism, magic, mentalism, audience management, and psychology — and on down the list it goes — improved exponentially faster than if I had to learn it all myself.

I got to learn from his decades of hard work and experience without actually having to go through it myself. He already knew what I wanted to know, so I didn't have to spend time figuring out where to find it; he was right there!

The same thing happened a couple years later when I went on tour with a full time entertainer for a year and a half. I was paid very little in terms of money, but I learned everything about making a business out of being a performer.

Now I get paid lots of money to teach other people the same thing. THey don't want to spend the time, so they have to spend the money.

And you can do the same for yourself. If you really want to learn something, find a mentor who is already doing exactly what it is that you want to do. Working closely with a mentor will turn your gradual line of progression on the graph of experience into an almost vertical line faster than you could ever believe.

Why?

Predigested information and immediate feedback

Like I said with Randi; he already knew everything I wanted to know. He also knew where I should start. He took all the guesswork out of where to go, what to find, and how to think about it.

Also, a mentor provides instant feedback.

Think about training a dog. Any trainer worth their salt will tell you to reward the behavior you want immediately after it happens. If you wait too long, the dog won't get the association between the right behavior and the reward for doing it. Instead, they'll just think, "Hey! Free treat!"

When there's immediate feedback, however, there's instant improvement. Plus, that's sometimes the only way you can learn something.

Pre-Radar Aircraft Detection

Imagine it's WWI and you want to know whether

those airplanes you hear in the distance are friendly, or foe.

If they're friendly and you scramble airplanes to intercept them, you've wasted precious fuel for no reason. If they're enemy aircraft and you don't scramble airplanes, you've just made a fatal error.

You need some system of 1) telling the difference between friend & foe, and 2) being able to do it as early as possible.

In 1916 Commander Alfred Rawlinson of the Royal Navy Reserve had the genius idea of using two gramophone horns to listen for approaching zeppelins. This allowed him to figure out where aircraft was approaching from farther away, in which direction, and even on cloudy days.

The idea took off, and with a quick search online of "WW1 airplane listening devices" you'll see all sorts of contraptions that developed from there.

The thing is, there were some people who were good

at discerning friend from foe, but not nearly enough people could do it. Leadership tried getting the people who could do it to create a training course to teach non-experts how to do it.

It didn't work.

Seemed like they were stuck. Then someone had a genius idea; have the experts and trainees work together directly.

Trainees would stand next to the experts, listen for an airplane, and then make their best guess. The expert would immediately tell them whether or not they were right. Before long, the trainee would be able to guess correctly with the same accuracy of the expert.

When asked how they could tell the difference, they'd say, "I don't know. It just feels right."

So what's going on?

Turns out the non-conscious mind is incredibly adept at recognizing patterns. That's what's helped us survive so long as a species. Those of our ancestors who were good at spotting the pattern of a tiger in the bushes would start running away sooner than those who couldn't.

This immediate expert/trainee feedback learning system can completely bypass the conscious mind and produce results that are simply impossible any other way.

That's why having a mentor is so absolutely vital to your success. Without direct instruction, immediate feedback, and guidance you can flounder for years working on something that could take a year, a month, a week, or even a day to learn with an expert's guidance.

Most of the success I've had in life began with a mentor's guidance to show me the right path to study, then put in the hard work to forge ahead myself. Without mentors like Randi, I don't know where I'd be. In order to learn the business of making a living doing shows, I toured with a full-time entertainer who was actively doing what I wanted to do. I worked with him for a year and a half to learn what I know. That information is vitally important to me, and not something I take lightly.

It's responsible for making me thousands and thousands of dollars as an entertainer, and it's opened doors to television, international tours, and more. That's why I know it's so valuable!

That's also why I spend thousands of dollars a year to work with coaches, trainers, and experts in whatever subject I'm interested in learning about. I know full well that if I were left to my own devices I could gain skills, but I can do it so much faster with a coach.

Further, that's why I chuckle to myself when anyone tells me they don't need a coach. I always reply with, "So you're better than every Olympic athlete in history? The highest performing people in the history of all mankind have coaches."

I'm usually met with silence.

So how do you get a coach?

Short answer is "be coachable."

Nobody wants to waste their time. Nobody wants to plant their seeds of wisdom in soil that's hostile to their growth. Demonstrate that you're the right soil. Demonstrate that you're willing to learn.

The best way to do that is to learn on your own. Show initiative.

Once a coach sees that you're already working on yourself, they can show you where to improve even more quickly. But they can't push you forward all by themselves.

They can show you the door, but you're the one who will have to walk through it. We're all judged by our actions, not our thoughts, wishes, hopes, or dreams.

What are you doing to improve your situation? That's what a coach is looking at.

So whatever the topic you're working on, find some-one who is already doing what you want to be doing, and then be willing to: 1) make it valuable to the expert in terms of time, money, etc to work with you 2) demonstrate a willingness to learn and initiative to work hard 3) actually listen to what they tell you. They're the expert; not you. You're paying them to teach you, not listen to your bellyaching.

It sounds harsh, but that's the truth. So many people think a coach's job is to listen to their problems.

That's the job of a therapist.

A coach's job is to take what you already have, and show you how to make it even more awesome. Coaches & mentors want to help your strengths get stronger.

Which is going to move you forward faster? Getting stronger where you naturally excel? Or trying to improve an area that you're not really good at?

Get better at what you're good at, and pay someone else to do the things for you that you aren't.

Do you want you and I to work together?

I'd be lying if I told you I'm not interested in working together. The fact that you've made it to the end of the book tells me you've found something valuable inside these pages.

(Or you have a compulsion like me that won't allow you to stop reading a book halfway through.)

Either way, I'd love to chat with you to see if we'd be a good fit to work together. Through the magic of the internet, we can be anywhere at any time with video conference calls.

Matter of fact, that's how I learned kung fu faster than any other student that my instructor had in the 20 years he's been teaching. But that's a story for another time.

Reach out. I want to hear from you. I want to figure out how I can help you put all that potential to maximum use. Let's work together and help you succeed like a mind reader!

Conclusion

Well, there you have it. Nearly (*wink*) all of my secrets about how I've learned all the skills that I use to create the life I want to lead.

No matter what topic or area of study you're thinking about, you'll find success if you apply the ideas you've just read.

Nothing makes me happier than knowing I've helped someone find their path. If you have success using something from this book, please let me know!

If you have challenges, I want to know that, too. I'd love to figure out how to help you get where you want to go.

Best thoughts,

~Jonathan Pritchard

Jonathan **Pritchard**

NOTES

About the Author

Jonathan Pritchard is a Mentalist, speaker, author, and coach for people who want to achieve the impossible in life, business, and relationships.

He was born in California, raised in North Carolina, went to college in Kentucky, spent his summers in Ft. Lauderdale, and has since lived in Orlando FL, Austin TX, and Chicago IL.

Most days he wakes up without an alarm, practices kung fu, has coffee, reads for an hour, has lunch with a friend, runs some errands, talks with clients, and then you could probably find him watching a movie.

When not on the road speaking or performing, you can find him in Chicago working on his podcast, website, and other adventures.

Made in the USA
Middletown, DE
05 August 2024

58524565R00071